STEPHEN A. DAVIS

JUST BEYOND GRIEF

Copyright © 2023 by Stephen A. Davis

Published by Kudu Publishing

All rights reserved. No portion of this book may be reproduced, stored in a retrieval system, or transmitted in any form or by any means—electronic, mechanical, photocopy, recording, scanning, or other—except for brief quotations in critical reviews or articles, without prior written permission of the author.

Scripture quotations marked MSG are taken from THE MESSAGE, copyright © 1993, 1994, 1995, 1996, 2000, 2001, 2002 by Eugene H. Peterson. Used by permission of NavPress. All rights reserved. Represented by Tyndale House Publishers, Inc. | Scripture quotations marked KJV are taken from the New King James Version®. Copyright © 1982 by Thomas Nelson. Used by permission. All rights reserved. | Scripture quotations marked NKJV are taken from the New King James Version®. Copyright © 1982 by Thomas Nelson. Used by permission. All rights reserved.

For foreign and subsidiary rights, contact the author.

Cover design by Ebbony E. Doty
Cover photo by Danny Kang Austin

ISBN: 978-1-960678-85-0   1 2 3 4 5 6 7 8 9 10

Printed in the United States of America

OTHER BOOKS BY STEPHEN A. DAVIS

Words To Inspire You To Dream

10 Years of Unprecedented Peace, Favor, and Abundance

I AM THE ONE

Master Your Fears: Kings Take Serpents By The Tail

Grief, Bishop Stephen Davis has taken a unique approach to tackling the topics of grief and loss, along with providing practical steps to help individuals and families to become healthy and whole. This is a must-read piece of work for not only those in the body of Christ but anyone who is in need of healing from the pain of grief and loss."

—Dr. Gloria Morrow
Licensed Clinical Psychologist
Director of Behavioral Health for Unicare
Community Health Center, Inc.

WHAT PEOPLE ARE SAYING ABOUT
JUST BEYOND GRIEF

"In the realm of spiritual guidance, few individuals possess the profound understanding and compassion of Apostle Stephen A. Davis. In his latest literary creation, each individual is invited to join in an enlightening journey of healing from the residue of sorrow. Drawing on his vast experience as a pastor, counselor, and spiritual father, Apostle Davis provides invaluable insight into understanding the situations that cause grief as well as navigating the complexities that accompany it.

Apostle Davis's book delves deep into the intricacies of grief, uncovering its various forms while offering practical advice on how to break free from its grip. His Holy Spirit-led and empathetic approach will serve as a guiding light for those grappling with loss. As you read, prepare for your eyes to be opened, your heart to be inspired, and your life to be transformed as the power of God uses the words of this book as an agent of change in your life. It is a high honor to be able to add my endorsement to this new work written by my trusted friend."

—Steve McCarty
Founding Pastor, Community Fellowship, Trussville, AL

"Many in the body of Christ are not mentally, physically, and spiritually healthy because of the unresolved grief and loss issues they are struggling to manage. In fact, far too many people of faith are suffering in silence. In the book *Just Beyond*

This book is dedicated to all the readers who have experienced some form of grief but now want to move Just Beyond Grief *and be reintroduced to God's plan for their lives.*

CONTENTS

Acknowledgments . . . . *xi*

CHAPTER 1. **Just Beyond Grief: There's Freedom** **13**

CHAPTER 2. **Just Beyond Grief: There's Healing** **21**

CHAPTER 3. **Just Beyond Grief: There's Victory Over Giants** **31**

CHAPTER 4. **Just Beyond Grief: There's Hope for The Future** **37**

CHAPTER 5. **Just Beyond Grief: Turn Your Grief Into Fuel Pt. 1** **41**

CHAPTER 6. **Just Beyond Grief: Turn Your Grief Into Fuel Pt. 2** **47**

CHAPTER 7. **Just Beyond Grief: Speaking Hope** **51**

ACKNOWLEDGMENTS

First, I would like to thank my wife, Darlene Davis, and our children, Sasha, Amber, and April, who always show their love and support in helping me to accomplish what God has set before me.

I would also like to express my sincere gratitude to those who gave their invaluable assistance and support during the course of publishing this book which has evolved into so much more!

Thank you to the licensed mental health professionals and Grief Recovery Team who provided valuable guidance and whose insights and expertise were instrumental in the success of this project. I am deeply grateful for their time and effort in helping me to accomplish this and the next phase of the movement.

Finally, I would like to extend my appreciation to the people who have expressed a need to recover from grief...

Because of their courage to make a change, this book was manifested.

CHAPTER 1

JUST BEYOND GRIEF: THERE'S FREEDOM

As with the children of Israel, you can always keep people bound who are still mourning the loss of great leadership. The children of Israel stayed in bondage to Pharaoh for 430 years because they were still mourning the loss of Joseph.

And Joseph said to his brethren, "I am dying; but God will surely visit you, and bring you out of this land to the land of which He swore to Abraham, to Isaac, and to Jacob." Then Joseph took an oath from the children of Israel, saying, "God will surely visit you, and you shall carry up my bones from here." So Joseph died, being one hundred and ten years old; and they embalmed him, and he was put in a coffin in Egypt. —Genesis 50:24-26 (NKJV)

A mind stuck in bondage will keep you from worshiping on the level of your potential. It is important to evolve through your worship. Oppressors are afraid of the worship of God's people. Pharaoh had a problem with the children of Israel worshipping God in Egypt. Because of this, Pharaoh released the children of Israel from bondage to go worship in Goshen. God then led them to Mount Sinai to worship Him in freedom. While you worship, God goes to battle for you. So, establish an altar of worship unto God and never allow for it to be taken away. Your altar is your time with God, the place you meet with God every day. As long as you have an altar of worship, you have victory and a God that shows up for you. If your altar cannot be removed, neither can your success. Freedom is at the altar.

HANNAH'S GRIEF

Then Elkanah her husband said to her, "Hannah, why do you weep? Why do you not eat? And why is your heart grieved? Am I not better to you than ten sons?" So Hannah arose after they had finished eating and drinking in Shiloh. Now Eli the priest was sitting on the seat by the doorpost of the tabernacle of the Lord. And she was in bitterness of soul, and prayed to the Lord and wept in anguish. Then she made a vow and said, "O Lord of hosts, if You will indeed look on the affliction of Your maidservant and remember me, and not forget Your maidservant, but will give Your maidservant a male child, then I will give him to the Lord all the days of his life, and no razor shall come upon his head." And it happened, as she continued praying before the Lord, that Eli watched her mouth. Now Hannah spoke in her heart; only her lips moved, but her voice was not heard. Therefore Eli thought she was drunk. So Eli said to her, "How long will you be drunk? Put your wine away from you!" But Hannah answered and said, "No, my lord, I am a woman of sorrowful spirit. I have drunk neither wine nor intoxicating drink, but have poured out my soul before the LORD. Do not consider your maidservant a wicked woman, for out of the abundance of my complaint and grief I have spoken until now." Then Eli answered and said, "Go in peace, and the God of Israel grant your petition which you have asked of Him." And she said, "Let your maidservant find favor in your sight." So the woman went her way and ate, and her face was no longer sad. —1 Samuel 1:8-18 (NKJV)

As scripture shows with Hannah, grief can make you unproductive in a fruitful time. Hannah had an issue with Peninnah, the second wife to their husband Elkanah, who would tease her for being childless. Regardless of her condition, Hannah's husband still loved her greatly and gifted her with many things. Having many *things,* however, does not exempt you from grieving what you don't have. You can have a lot of stuff, but not what you desire.

Because Peninnah was not carrying the spirit of grief, she was able to produce multiple children. She is an example that expansion is automatic when you are free from grief. Know that grief is capable of blocking you from functioning at the capacity that you should function. Hannah cried out for what she needed and was in anguish for what she wanted. Although she asked for what she desired, she still grieved for it. As the Bible states, "ye have not, because ye ask not" (KJV, James 4:2). So yes, you may be asking, but what's blocking you from receiving?

Concerning the church, if Satan wants to stop your production, he will aim to keep you in grief. The church has to start addressing grief effectively because the gifts that will prophesy to nations are in the church. Satan's tactic is to move the church into grief so that it never births a prophet but remember redemption to nations is in the church.

Grief knows how fertile (productive) you can be if you get over your anguish. The thing you want, and what God is trying to release through you, is already in you. You are carrying too much good to allow negative events to hinder and block what God wants to bring into your life.

Therefore, to be productive, you have to be determined to be grief free. Satan would have to block you inwardly to stop you. In her determination, Hannah set her grief and anguish aside to make a deal with God to dedicate her son fully to Him. In doing this, Eli the priest saw Hannah praying to God but did not understand and instead assumed she was drunk. Church leaders should be able to properly pick up on the hearts of those in communication with God and the hearts of those grieving. "For man looketh on the outward appearance, but the Lord looketh on the heart" (KJV, 1 Samuel 16:7). God heard Hannah's heart and rewarded her heart by giving her, her heart's desire. When you posture yourself correctly, God will hear you and in your conversation with God, He will raise you up. Hannah dedicated her child to serving the purpose of God only. She understood that if you get away from purpose, you lose your existence. Always remember the conversations you've had in your heart with God and realign yourself so that your purpose remains activated.

The same purpose that opened the womb once, will also provide space for all that will come after. When you have dedicated the first fruit to the Lord it is hard to be singular in productivity.

Every out-of-the-box thing that God does is proof that if you make a significant level of commitment to Him, He will make a much more exceeding level of commitment to you. After her commitment to God, Hannah was no longer grieving even though she still showed no signs of pregnancy. You have to know, not just think, that grief is over. If you are in anguish, it is because you have been in expectation for a long time, and nothing has happened. Therefore, when you are unable to produce, even though you are doing everything to produce, it begins to impact you intellectually. Know that your Father God still loves you in your non-productive state. You must, however, be bold enough to attack what has been attacking you. God is releasing you to go to the highest level of productivity and to get back pay for at least three generations of non-productive people. The former and the latter rain will come at once. The time to push is now.

CHAPTER 2

JUST BEYOND GRIEF: THERE'S HEALING

Grief can cause you to abort the plan of God for your life. We can be under the impression that everything is good but, if we cannot perform the simple things that are asked of us, it is not good. Satan has always functioned in the spirit of deception. You can't just deal with the spirit of grief in the intellectual realm. It's the anointing that helps people who don't even know they are grieving.

Through the inspiration of the Holy Spirit and the revealing of truth, we have to know what God is saying in this season. Grief is the real enemy, showing itself as division amongst siblings and spouses, sickness in the body, grief over moving from one location to the next, and even grief over an empty nest. When grieving, it is wise to wait a year before making a major decision so that you avoid making the wrong decision. You cannot depend on the emotions of someone who is in grief. Because of this, leadership should not consist of hurting, sick, or grieving people, they instead need a place to heal.

DAVID'S GRIEF

2 Samuel 12:15-24

Grief will lead to depression and behaviors that are unbecoming if it goes unaddressed. A good person in continuous grief can turn into a wicked person. Take note that when you are in a grieving place you have to be willing to listen and show respect to God's servant. As we see with David, he showed respect to the prophet Nathan even when his mind was not intact. David's grief may go beyond Bathsheba and the loss of his son and into the moment he was called forth last amongst his brothers (KJV, 1 Samuel 16:1-13). Be aware that grief can grab hold of you while you are in a place of waiting. David may also have been grieving the fact that his mother's name was never mentioned in the Word.

His unhealed grief could be what led to him taking Bathsheba, who did not belong to him. The message that the prophet Nathan delivered to David, regarding the future death of his child was difficult for him to hear because he was used to having everything he wanted. Ultimately, not only was David grieving his child's illness, but David was also grieving over the consequence of a wrong decision he'd made out of his emotions. David was a king, but he wasn't whole.

David pleaded with God for his child to live. He then took on the posture of grief and he refused to eat or get up. Note that there is often additional grief that comes from praying and hoping but not receiving the desired results. Grief can cause a refusal to rise up or to maintain a healthy diet. It has the ability to keep you down when people want you to get up and can even result in a change in your patterns of behavior and mood. Grief can start before the anticipated disappointment takes place. Notice in scripture, David began to grieve before his child died. I once experienced this same reaction before my father, who was ill at the time, transitioned. Although he was still alive and within an eye gaze away, I began to weep because I didn't want to lose my father. After he transitioned, I didn't shed a tear, I had already grieved. In scripture we see that after David receives the verdict that his child has died, he rises up, washes his face, anoints himself, and changes clothes. As a leader, you are ahead of the people, even in grief. Know that grieving, for a certain period of time, is healthy. But the spirit of grief isn't a holy spirit, there is no way we can keep it. Extended grief will keep you from loving your brothers and sisters because the last thing that was close to you died, and you don't want to get close to anyone else. This thought pattern is a sign that you are still grieving and still in the same place where the event that caused it occurred.

Anytime you detest worship, it is because you are grieving something you haven't overcome. When "You're the One," there is a desire to go worship once the grief has ended. You cannot worship God and focus on grief because whatever you put your focus on, that is what you worship.

Grief can push you into the arms of God or the hands of the adversary. Worship is automatic when you aren't grieving. God created man for worship, but this must be an anointed worship so that those who are grieving are lifted when they enter the House of Worship. In 1 Samuel 30: 1-7 (KJV), we see David operate in this anointing by putting on his ephod and changing his posture when the people wanted to kill him in Ziklag. In your worst moments, you must put on your anointing. Know that the instruction isn't to avoid grief, the instruction is to grieve well and then put on the anointing. To do great things you have to have the power of endurance on your life.

Worship involves a restoration of intimacy which produces new life. While you are grieving you should worship. If you don't worship, there is no intimacy with the God who impregnates you with new life. Intimacy is "In-To-Me-See." You have to get close enough to God so that into you He sees and then you can discern your condition. You cannot discern your condition until you worship God. Praise is one thing; it correlates to cheers at sporting events and activities but worship correlates to one-on-one intimacy.

To gain new life you have to leave the old behind. Don't block the new thing that God wants to bring into your life with an old mentality. Every time you experience grief get ready for a new life, fresh vision, more than enough, double and increase everywhere. Only grief causes you to believe that you cannot recover, but you shall recover. The reason you survived the grief is because you will go back and deliver those who are still in it. The anointing will raise you up.

Over time I have discovered that grief is a major problem in the body of Christ and the world at large. Most people, however, do not know how to diagnose grief. You must understand that you can experience many events in life which cause grief and not even know you are grieving. An empty nest, loss of mobility through illness, divorce or separation, demotion on the job, and even a lost opportunity can all cause grief. It would be an injustice to go without addressing these issues that are hindering the advancement of the church.

Many have labeled church people as some of the meanest people on earth, without understanding they were in grief without the space to be healed. It is important to realize that everyone processes differently, you can't "just get over it." With my involvement in the lives of many people, I have been able to see the behavior patterns of people change and shift over time. I have seen people go from excited and bubbly to seemingly depressed and withdrawn and I can often trace these shifts back to devastation or disappointment in their lives. Understanding this, I conduct myself differently knowing that I am dealing with people who are grieving both current and past events, not just people who are troubled. Anything negative that happens to you impacts your life. People may encourage you to "just get up and move on" but as we see in scripture, that wasn't even easy for King David. Grief has a way of fastening you down to where only those with the anointing can raise you up. There is nothing wrong with identifying with grief especially if the anointing is near and you are receptive to what it takes to get you out of that grieving place.

The unfortunate issue in the church is that everyone is grieving, from the top to the bottom. Leadership within the church has to get healthy. Hypothetically, doctors and nurses cannot run out of the emergency room, into the lobby area and ask for help for themselves. If the doctors and nurses are asking for help and the patients are needing help, no one has help. Grief can begin to numb you to where you lack compassion and aren't sensitive to your pain or the pain of others. So, in knowing this, room to grieve has to be created for those who are seeking healing. The Bible states it was with compassion that Jesus healed them (KJV, Matthew 14:14). Never throw a person away who is seeking healing.

Understand that people are not coming to the church because everything was perfect in their past. To move on, something has to end, even if it is God that brought it to an end. So, know that if you were in that old place for a while, you created some level of attachment or relationship. In detaching, even if the relationship was distasteful, there is grief.

CHAPTER 3

JUST BEYOND GRIEF: THERE'S VICTORY OVER GIANTS

When grief comes, if not diagnosed properly, it will take your zeal away. Grief is a tool of Satan to take the fight out of the body of Christ.

GOLIATH IS GRIEF

2 Samuel 17:20-27, 1 Thessalonians 4:13, Luke 4:18

Grief is not isolated to just your home. Grief is both a national and global spiritual enemy. Understand that while monitored grief can be positive, without monitorization or boundaries, grief can be deadly. Death from grief occurs in layers. If you grieve long enough you become depressed and if you stay depressed long enough you become suicidal. Remember grief is a spiritual enemy, you cannot overcome the spirit of grief by natural means. You attack the spiritual with the spiritual. Just as in worship, when you worship; worship in spirit and truth because without spirit there is no truth. God never intended for a worship service to be natural, worship services should be spiritual because of the one you are worshiping.

There is currently a wave of disappointment in the body of Christ where carnality has been introduced through a lack of accountability. The mindset that the church does not have to report to anyone, leaves the church without headship, and without headship in the church, there is no command center. Without headship, people are subject to experiences they normally wouldn't have if there were headship in place. I know the anointing on my life and the ministry is to bring down the giant of grief that threatens God's people. Whenever God was ready to move the church forward, He raised up headship. Before delivering Israel, God sent Moses. Before leading Israel into the Promise Land, He sent Joshua. When God wanted to liberate Israel, He raised up Gideon.

When He wanted to deal with the Philistines, He raised up Samson who slayed them with the jawbone of a donkey. When God was ready to deliver the children of Israel, He raised up Esther and when He wanted to deliver the people from the flood, He raised up Noah. Nowhere in the Bible did the church move forward without headship.

So, someone has to be raised up to speak to the spirit of grief, but this requires consecration because grief will expose you. When the enemy wants to destroy the church, he tries to expose weaknesses and bring dirt on the leader. Your history has to be impeccable before you confront something like grief, so when people gossip, they have nothing to validate their claims. That's why when you have good headship you must support them and pray for them. We see in scripture both Saul and God were ready to reward whoever brought down the spirit of grief that was Goliath (1 Samuel 17:25). Understand that the God in heaven and the earthly government gives reward to the person or groups that remove the challenge. It doesn't make sense to be anointed and flee. Notice David didn't badger his brothers for being scared, he simply took care of what they wouldn't.

1 Thessalonians 4:13 (MSG), encourages us that the grave doesn't have the last word. In this passage of scripture, the Apostle Paul addresses the concerns of the Thessalonian church regarding the return of Christ and those who die before His return. The Thessalonian church believed that any believer who died before the return of Christ missed out on something. They thought there was a disadvantage to death for believers

of Christ and so they grieved just as those who were not in Christ. The Apostle Paul wanted the church to know that as believers, we face the loss of loved ones in hope. Those in Christ don't grieve over those who were born again as if they didn't know Christ.

As believers, after death, there is hope and assurance of resurrection. How many things have you grieved over that God has a replacement for? If you are still grieving over your losses, you have not yet made room for the things that will come in your life that are better.

Grief only has you because you are not knowledgeable about the thing you are grieving about. So, we must have anointed, God-sent, God-fearing people who will spend time to find the truth, or else we will live a lie. The truth is that everything in Christ gets up again, your resurrection day has come.

CHAPTER 4

JUST BEYOND GRIEF: THERE'S HOPE FOR THE FUTURE

Jeremiah 29:11 (NKJV)

"For I know the thoughts that I think toward you, says the LORD, thoughts of peace and not of evil, to give you a future and a hope."

Suffering will always produce an unusual harvest if you process it correctly. Pressure, pain, rejection, naysayers, and criticism are all ingredients for multiplication and growth. According to scripture, "The more they afflicted them the more they multiplied and grew...." (Exodus 1:12, KJV).

Grief hinders you from seeing or believing in the future. People often think that the negative events that took place in their life ended their opportunity to move forward. Think about it, God was elevating Jesus while the people were crucifying Him. In reference to His crucifixion, Jesus stated "And I, if I be lifted up from the earth, will draw all men unto me." (KJV, John 12:32). It is when people crucify you that you gain more influence. Everyone has their personal opinion about you, and it has no value. Prioritize what God thinks about you.

When the thoughts of God are preached, grief begins to lose its hold. Receive the good news that the old day is over, and a new day has begun. Know that there is something great beyond your grief and suffering. Divorce yourself from the bad season and embrace the good season. Once you hear what God thinks, nothing else matters. You may be carrying what others negatively thought or spoke about you so release yourself from what *they* say. There is a day coming that the Lord promised you and no negative event in your life can wipe it away. Begin to see and think about yourself the way God sees and thinks about you. You are on God's mind for the future. If you dwell on the past you will miss God, He's only concerned about what you are about to do.

Don't rehearse a nightmare when you are in a dream. Joseph's dream is what kept him alive after 13 years of living in a nightmare. So, when you are in your dark times, don't give up, it is an announcement that good times are on the way. Your future is better than your past.

Don't ask God to clean up your past, ask him to prepare you for your future. Understand that you went down as a seed, but you are coming up as a tree. You had to be buried to germinate. The Word makes it clear; you need a root system in order to flourish, (Psalms 92:13-15).

God has planned a peaceful future for you. When peace is around, the storms are temporary. If peace is a part of your future, don't give up on the middle ground, you're almost there. Whenever your peace is threatened by something or someone, it's because it sees your future. The enemy will attack your mind because, in the future, your mind will work for you. Your mind holds a strategy for the advancement of mankind, keep your focus. In all times keep your hope in God. Understand that the thing that is holding you cannot move forward with you. Don't wrestle with things that are already defeated, use your energy for your future. The further you go, the more strongholds that will be broken. God saved you for the future he has for you. In the words of minister Frederick J. Eikerenkoetter (Reverend Ike), "I just can't lose with the stuff I use."

CHAPTER 5

JUST BEYOND GRIEF: TURN YOUR GRIEF INTO FUEL PT. 1

1 Peter 5:10, Luke 22:31-32

Satan always asks for what God has called into purpose, but no matter how much Satan has asked for you, God has already purposed you. You may have made decisions that are not supportive of your destiny, but the grief you carry for those mistakes has become fuel for your future. God will use that trash to fuel you for your future. You may mistakenly think your fuel comes from a perfect situation, but fuel comes from negative situations. God will restore and repair whatever is damaged, so the believer will be able to face whatever lies ahead. When God brings restoration in your life you are now strong enough to handle what lies ahead. God is prepping you and preparing you so you can handle what is ahead.

Don't let what the enemy throws at you grieve you so badly that you can't face your future. Prepare for what's ahead of you, not behind you. God will rekindle your faith and hope. Whatever didn't kill you although it hurt or was unexpected will fuel you. There is a component of suffering that goes along with the journey. But right behind the turbulence, God will perfect, establish and settle you. Failure in the past does not doom you to failure in the future. As with Peter, we see that he suffered and failed in the past, but it did not doom him. Not only does it not doom you, it sets you up for success in the future. Keep believing even though you are grieving. In the middle of storms and chaos, you can see God's hand at work.

Restoration means the repairing and refitting of a damaged boat or in the medical sense, the setting of a broken bone. God is going to repair you from all the grief and damage. For some, the pressure of grief fractures you so the resetting now allows you to anticipate full function. God will never repair unless what He repairs will function at a high capacity. After this (grief), you will be much higher in your operation, you will see and experience more in your life. Know that God doesn't repair in the way others repair. After most repairs, you have to avoid pressure or only apply a certain amount of weight but with God, you will be able to handle more. There is a restoration and repair taking place in your life because what you thought would cancel you out set you up for your future. In scripture we see, after God brought the disciples back from running away in doubt, He filled them with the Holy Spirit, and they were better than when they were walking with Jesus. You are better because you have been repaired by God.

Many people think life is over when they experience loss but there will be restoration and a future. God will make followers of Christ stronger, more stable and He will provide them with the courage to go on. In times of grieving people often question whether they can go on. You can move on. There is strength, courage, and stability for you, no matter what tries to take your courage, God has prepared you for it. Your future is already established and there is nothing the enemy can do about it. Your destiny is settled. You have to be settled in your future. When you are settled, the devil is wasting his time by bringing negative circumstances into your life. Jesus had to pray for Peter to be settled. Once you are settled, it is a losing game for anyone to try and change your mind. Grief tends to unsettle you, so for every moment of grief you experience, fortify that area. Allow the challenges from your past to teach you how to structure your future. Every force that has been working against you is broken. God will make us firm and steadfast so that our foundation in him is secure. No matter how shaky your past has been, God will make you firm and steadfast because He is getting ready to build on you. The Bible mentions two houses, one built on sand and one built on a rock. A storm came to both houses, the one built on sand fell greatly but the one built on a rock did not. You can only find security in Jesus Christ. When you turn your grief into fuel, you will get to your promise a lot faster. Your future cannot be voided out, you just need to show up for it.

CHAPTER 6

JUST BEYOND GRIEF: TURN YOUR GRIEF INTO FUEL PT. 2

1 Peter 5:10, Luke 22:31-32

In scripture, we see where Peter made it through the moments when Satan requested to have him. Because of the testing Peter experienced in these moments, he was able to be highly productive on the day of Pentecost. 1 Peter 5:10 begins with "After you have suffered *a little while*". Many people see "a while" as a long period of time but by definition, "a while" is a small or little period of time. If you have experienced suffering, grief, or sorrow, you have already suffered for a small or little period of time and God is ready to do something amazing.

After this small period of suffering, God will perfect you. Perfect means to restore. Know that whatever you lose, God will perfect you, meaning He will restore you. He will fit and join together everything that was disassembled. You will be brought back together with one mind and a restored soul. Perfecting also represents "adjustment" or the putting of all parts into the right relation or connection. In Ezekiel 37, it speaks about The Valley of Dry Bones which was restored to become a vast army, in right relation and connection. After you have suffered for a while, everything will come together on your behalf. If you process the small period of grief correctly, perfection will come, restoration will come, a proper fitting together will come, adjustments will come, and right relations and connections will come. Every trauma and damage in your mind will be restored.

If you pay attention to a light bulb that has blown or gone bad and lost its light, look inside. If it's clear, you can see where the filament was disconnected causing an interruption in the circuit and no production of light. Metaphorically, in your life God is rejoining the electrical filament that was broken by grief, so now you can create light. This rejoining and reconnecting turns your purpose and dreams back on. 1 Peter 5:10 also states that Christ will establish you. The word establish is the root word of the word steadfast which means firmly fitted in place. God will fit you in a place where you will not be moved. Some events will take place and statements will be made that may have moved you before but will no longer move you now that you have been established. When you are firmly fitted in place, you no longer fluctuate in your thinking. Grief fuels stability when processed correctly. 1 Peter 5:10 goes on to state that Christ will strengthen you. Understand that to strengthen means to make stronger continuously, not just to make strong once. At a certain point you will become stronger than your opposition. Once Christ has perfected you, established you, and strengthened you He will also settle you which means to cause you to come to rest. It is hard to rest with grief breathing down your neck but now that a small period of time has passed God will settle you. You will be resting in your mind, in your heart, spiritually and physically. People think that things weaken over a period of time, but we see in scripture where Simon who became Peter went from being shaky to becoming a rock that God could build His church on. Peter became so settled that while in jail, a place considered bondage, he took a nap (Acts 12: 5-17). Your suffering has not weakened you it has strengthened you and settled you.

CHAPTER 7

JUST BEYOND GRIEF: SPEAKING HOPE

Ezekiel 37:1-14, 1 Corinthians 1:21

God is doing a major restoration process in the body of Christ, specifically with individuals who have been oppressed in any way. With Ezekiel, we see where God touched him and caused him to speak to the hopeless. In the church, so much has happened in the body of Christ that we no longer believe there will be an experience when we come to worship. But heaven is capable of opening over your life. As a leader, when the presence of the Holy Spirit comes on me it isn't just for me to shout, it is for me to exercise authority and power so the marginalized can embrace the fullness of what heaven has to offer. Most people have only experienced what their parents have taught them but there is more and greater to be embraced. There is a certain sound that no matter how dead you are, will cause you to rise again. Know that God always raises up a deliverer from among the people. To understand the people, you have to have experienced what they've experienced.

As we see in scripture, when the man of God began to speak, the dry bones came together (Ezekiel 37:1-14). God's hand will rest on the prophet when it's time to bring the structure together. Whenever you walk into a company or community and cannot tell who the leader is, that's a sign that things are scattered. The devil loves for things to be scattered because it is a sign that there is no hope. If the church structure is out of balance the power of God cannot flow. It's not God if there are deficits in one area of the body of Christ and increases in other areas.

God's hand has to rest on someone in order to bring structure. Nothing is successful without structure. Whenever God gets ready to do something major, he raises up an anointed leader. The prophet must begin to function in his divinity and not his humanity. Leaders, understand that you cannot facilitate the Holy Word of God in your humanity or else you will promote your opinion instead of God's truth. When you are in divinity, the opposition cannot rule, and dry bones respond. If you do not consecrate before you minister you will be ineffective. The saying "Lord, less of us all of you" is an example of moving into divinity and leaving humanity.

We are commanded to prophesy or preach the gospel because it brings hope. When you are talking to a scattered people you must have the command from God, so they are empowered to act. It is necessary to echo the commands of Heaven on Earth, which point to your future. When you are in divinity you have insight regarding things that the average intellectual mind has not comprehended. God commanded Ezekiel to tell the dry bones that their future was filled with breath and life. When you are in divinity you don't call it as it is, you call it as God says it will be. Everyone with a past has a future. You have to understand who you are talking to when you are handling people. The problems we have in our communities are due to not having a prophet to speak life. Under passive leadership, the enemy can rule over your life. If every joint supplies, we can join together to put a command on the enemy to leave our possessions and the next generation alone. God's hand is resting heavily on the life of his servant to bring life to his body (army). Don't forget who you are. Just because you walk through the valley doesn't mean you have to create your bed there. Whenever you see a heavy anointing on a leader it's because there is a people that God wants to live. It takes a word for your future to get you through the adversity of your present. You may have been misjudged by others or misjudged yourself, but all the bad judgment can't cancel God's plan for your life.

www.ingramcontent.com/pod-product-compliance
Lightning Source LLC
Chambersburg PA
CBHW070050100426
42734CB00040B/2969